WHILE THERE WERE no members of any Native tribe at the Berkeley Thanksgiving in 1619, the Chickahominy Tribe were among the first to welcome European settlers to these shores. Therefore, it is fitting that I be the first to welcome readers to this often-overlooked tale of our nation's first English-speaking Thanksgiving in America.

At the heart of this book, you will see a Chickahominy dance circle. The ritual dance is a form of thanks and praise for the Creator. As long as the river bearing our name has been flowing to the sea, the Chickahominy Indian Tribe has been a part of this great nation. For more than 400 years, we have extended the hand of fellowship and hospitality.

At long last, we can give thanks for our tribe being recognized by the federal government. I am grateful to all those who worked tirelessly to make this happen. It is gratifying to know legislative bodies of this land we call Turtle Island unanimously acknowledge the sovereignty of the Chickahominy People who have lived here for millennia.

We remain proud of our heritage, our place in this land and the intricate cultural dance we continue to perform hand-in-hand as a nation.

Stephen Adkins

Chief of the Chickahominy Indian Tribe

THANKS TO THE SUPPORT of Warren Stewart we have this book that allows me to honor our history. It is his wish that we remember to nourish the hungry by supporting our local food banks and support sheltering our homeless throughout the year.

In gratitude to all the good stewards of our nation's history. In memory of those throughout that history who suffered in bondage to poverty, hunger and other cruel masters.

For the best part of my personal history - My husband Robert Suhay and our children, Zoltan, Ian, Avery, Quin and Elizabeth.

Lisa Suhay

First edition, published in Norfolk, Virginia, by Mermaid Media
ISBN-13: 978-1722018818
Text Copyright © 2018 by Lisa Suhay
Illustrations Copyright © 2018 by Savyra Meyer-Lippold
Book design by Robert Suhay

America
the Grateful

Where Thanksgiving really began

SOMEONE call the president.
We've got to set the record straight,
on everything about Thanksgiving,
from the date to what they ate.

HANG ON tight.
Here's the tale that's right.
You're in for quite a shock:
The first day of thanks happened in Virginia,
not Plymouth Rock.

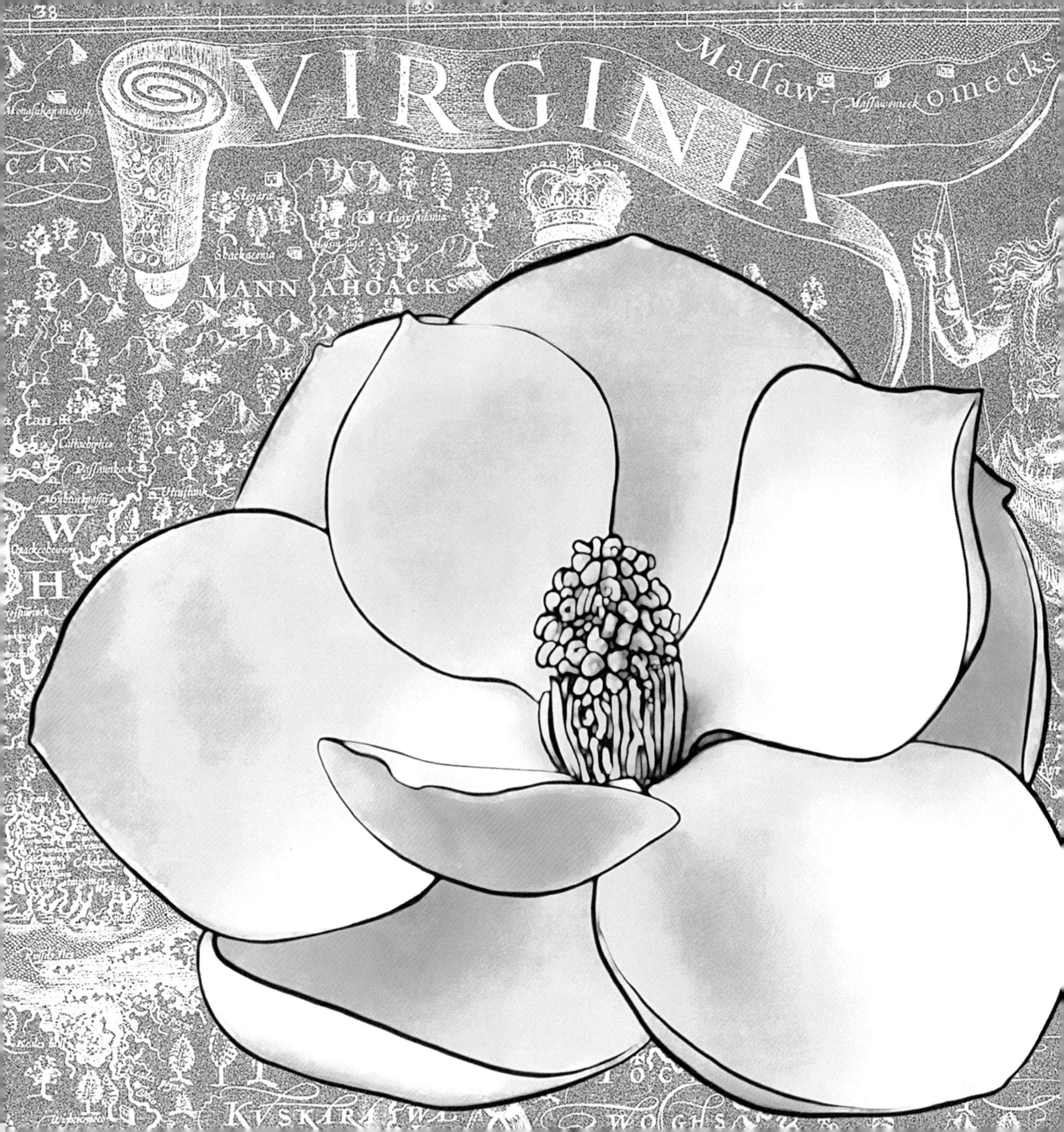
VIRGINIA
MANN AHOACKS

I T WASN'T in November.
Turkey wasn't on the table.
They ate ham, oysters
and anything they were able.

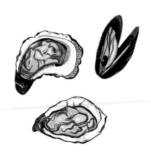

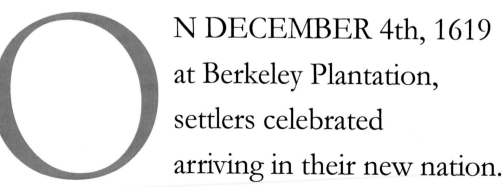

N DECEMBER 4th, 1619
at Berkeley Plantation,
settlers celebrated
arriving in their new nation.

THEIR MEAL wasn't like
the ones we do today.
Nobody watched a parade
or a football team play.
They didn't do much cooking,
what they really did was pray.

C APTAIN John Woodlief got orders
from the Berkeley Company
for settlers all to gather 'round
and give thanks on bended knee.

Dec. 4, 1

We ordain that
the day of
our ship's arrival
at the place assigned
for plantation
in the land of
Virginia
shall be yearly and
perpetually kept holy
as a day of
thanksgiving to
Almighty God.

619

T

HEY GAVE THANKS to God
for their safe trip across a stormy sea.

Today we can say thanks for many things
in a land where we're all free.

THANKS for neighbors
of every creed and color,
for friends and family.
Thanks for teachers who set us straight.
Thanks for firefighters who are never late.
Thanks for every happy minute.
Thanks for a kitchen with food in it.
Thanks for everything we've got,
even when it's not a lot.

IT DOESN'T matter if we're eating turkey or tofu. As long as we've got the freedom to be me and you. From shore to shore, let's make gratitude more of what this holiday celebrates across our nation, just like they did at Berkeley Plantation.

I F WE FOCUS on an attitude of gratitude,
the mood and not the food,
then from fall to fall,
we can share an America
that is both beautiful and grateful for all.

Some notable Virginians

1 Thomas Jefferson

April 13, 1743 – July 4, 1826

Founding father; principal author of the Declaration of Independence; third U.S. president, 1801 to 1809.

2 Dred Scott

c. 1799 – Sept. 17, 1858

Enslaved African American; unsuccessfully sued for his freedom and that of his wife and two daughters in 1857.

3 Stephen Adkins

Dec. 3, 1945

Chief of The Chickahominy Indian Tribe, first elected in 2001. Advocate for federal recognition of the tribe.

4 Michael Twitty

March 20, 1977

Author of "The Cooking Gene: A Journey Through African-American Culinary History in the Old South."

5 Pearl Bailey

March 29, 1918 – Aug. 17, 1990

Actress, singer; received the Screen Actors Guild Life Achievement Award and Presidential Medal of Freedom.

6 James Madison

March 16, 1751 – June 28, 1836

Founding father; fourth U.S. president, 1809 to 1817. Took pivotal role in drafting the Constitution, Bill of Rights.

7 Booker T. Washington

c.1856 – Nov. 14, 1915

Educator, author, orator and advisor to presidents; leader among African Americans from1890 to 1915.

8 Lyon Gardiner Tyler

August 24, 1853 – Feb. 12, 1935

Educator, lawyer, state delegate, genealogist and historian; the fourth son of President John Tyler.

9 Malcom E. and Grace Jamieson

Responsible for the restoration of Berkeley Plantation, the site of the first Thanksgiving and birthplace of U.S. president William Henry Harrison.

10 Maggie L. Walker

July 15, 1864 – Dec. 15, 1934

African-American teacher and businesswoman; first female bank president to charter a bank in the United States. Limited to a wheelchair later in life, she became an example for people with disabilities.

11 George Washington

Feb. 22, 1732 – Dec. 14, 1799

Founding father, statesman and soldier; first U.S. president, 1789 to 1797. Commander-in-chief of the Continental Army during the American Revolutionary War; presided over the 1787 convention that drafted the Constitution.

Flora and fauna at Berkeley

The American Dogwood
Cornus florida

Virginia adopted the shapely bloom as its state flower in 1918. It's also the state's official tree since 1956.

The English Boxwood
Buxus sempervirens

Its slow growth makes the wood hard and well suited for cabinets, tools and musical instruments.

The Southern Magnolia
Magnolia grandiflora

An evergreen tree which may grow 120 feet tall and generally has a pyramidal shape.

The Hackberry Tree
Celtis occidentalis

Its leaves have a distinctive serrated edge and its berries begin orange-red and ripen to a deep purple.

The Cardinal
Cardinalis cardinalis

Virginia's state bird since 1950, both males and females sing. The males have distinctive red plumage.

The Redbud
Cercis canadensis

The tree's magenta flowers appear in clusters from spring to early summer, even before the leaves.

The Weeping Mulberry
Morus alba

The species is native to northern China and was cultivated to feed silkworms. It hybridizes easily with the native red mulberry.

The Cedar
Juniperus virginiana

The eastern juniper, or red cedar, is a hearty tree that is often first to repopulate cleared land and may live for more than 900 years.

The Hardy Orange
Citrus trifoliata

Unusual among citrus for having deciduous, compound leaves and downy fruit, debate lingers whether it should have its own genus.

Thanks, from Berkeley Plantation

I N FEBRUARY 1619, the Virginia Company of London granted four adventurers 8,000 acres along the King James River in the colony of Virginia. These adventurers who made up the Berkeley Company were William Throckmorton, John Smyth, George Thorpe, and Richard Berkeley. They recruited 35 crew members and appointed John Woodlief captain and leader of the expedition.

On September 16, 1619, the Good Ship Margaret left Bristol, England to cross the ocean with Captain Woodlief and his men headed to the New World. After a stormy voyage across the Atlantic, the ship and its passengers landed at Berkeley Hundred on December 4, 1619.

On that day, Captain Woodlief and his men held a religious service in accordance with specific instructions given in the charter by the Berkeley Company, which declared:

"We ordain that the day of our ship's arrival, at the place assigned for plantation, in the land of Virginia, shall be yearly and perpetually kept holy as a day of thanksgiving to Almighty God."

The first official English-speaking Thanksgiving in the New World had just occurred.

In 1620, more settlers arrived at Berkeley. The settlement grew and peacefully developed until 1622. Just over two years after the landing, an Indian uprising abruptly ended the settlement of Berkeley and the annual Thanksgiving ceremony.

Photograph by P. Kevin Morley, Richmond Times-Dispatch

The history of the first Thanksgiving was lost for many centuries until Dr. Lyon Tyler, son of President John Tyler and retired president of The College of William and Mary, discovered the records in 1931. He made his discovery known to his young neighbor, Malcolm Jamieson, who had taken up residence at Berkeley only a few years earlier.

In 1958, the annual celebration of Thanksgiving was reborn thanks to the efforts of Virginia Senator John Wicker. In that same year, the Jamiesons invited members of the Woodlief family to the plantation to observe the annual event. That was the beginning of the Virginia Thanksgiving Festival, as we know it today.

Every year on the first Sunday of November, Berkeley Plantation hosts the Virginia Thanksgiving Festival. Visitors enjoy an afternoon immersed in the history of early colonial America with a parade, fife and drum performers, first person re-enactors, arts and crafts vendors, colonial games, performances by local tribal dancers, and a reenactment of America's First Thanksgiving on the banks of the James River where Captain Woodlief and his crew landed 400 years ago.

Virginia Thanksgiving Festival, Inc. would like to thank Dr. Warren Stewart and members of the Woodlief/Woodliff family for the generous contributions made to help with the continued recognition and celebration of America's First Thanksgiving.

Join us annually on the first Sunday in November at Berkeley Plantation in Charles City, Virginia for the celebration of America's First Thanksgiving.

Virginia Thanksgiving Festival, Inc.,
c/o Berkeley Plantation
12602 Harrison Landing Road,
Charles City, Va. 23030
www.virginiathanksgivingfestival.com, www.berkeleyplantation.com, (804) 829-6018

Afterword

Gratitude of a Founding Father

 A RISING NATION, spread over a wide and fruitful land, traversing all the seas with the rich productions of their industry, engaged in commerce with nations who feel power and forget right, advancing rapidly to destinies beyond the reach of mortal eye … possessing a chosen country, with room enough for our descendants to the thousandth and thousandth generation … enlightened by a benign religion, professed, indeed, and practiced in various forms, yet all of them inculcating honesty, truth, temperance, gratitude, and the love of man; acknowledging and adoring an overruling Providence, which by all its dispensations proves that it delights in the happiness of man here and his greater happiness hereafter – with all these blessings, what more is necessary to make us a happy and a prosperous people?"

Thomas Jefferson

From his first Inaugural Address, March 4, 1801
Words selected by Clay Jenkinson

About "The Thomas Jefferson Hour"

A weekly conversation with America's third president as portrayed by Clay Jenkinson. To learn more about the program, visit www.jeffersonhour.com.

About the selection

THOMAS JEFFERSON was a revolutionary, a visionary, a pragmatic utopian, and the greatest articulator of the American Dream. He understood that America must always be about possibility and abundance.

He was the father of the concept of American exceptionalism – that we are somehow different from all the other peoples of the world. He was not a perfect man, but he firmly believed that the sovereign American people are equal to the challenge of self-government and that the future will always be better than the past and present.

He believed that there is no birthright equal to being born in America, and that average Americans would show the world what liberty and the pursuit of happiness can be on earth.

Clay Jenkinson

American Humanities scholar,
co-host of "The Thomas Jefferson Hour"

❝ TO ME, love and gratitude move the world forward and turn lives around - I am honored and grateful to have been involved with this book."

❝ I HOPE this book will give families a fresh reason to stop, read and discuss the meaning of gratitude together."

Savyra Meyer-Lippold

The illustrator, designer and screenwriter lives in Cape Town, South Africa, where she runs on kefir, red wine and coffee.

Lisa Suhay

The author is a career journalist, who has written for The New York Times and The Christian Science Monitor. This is her 10th book, including "There Goes a Mermaid: A NorFolktale," "Tell Me a Story" and "Dreamcatchers."

Faces of "Gratitude"

The author would like to thank the children and adults who lent their images to the illustrations: Mila Chzasz-Lopez; Jaxin, Symin, Linkin and Quin Dawson; Jack and Robert Evans; Heather Barlow; Langston Fauntleroy; Jayden Foreman; Nia Hugely; Vinnie Lanier; Marquis and Jahari Parker; Natalia and Chyna Robins; Logan Rome; Warren Stewart; Giovanni Giorgio Sykes; and Lera and Omnia.

93242450R00020

Made in the USA
Lexington, KY
13 July 2018